The House of Green

Natural Homes and Biophilic Architecture

gestalten

BUILDING WITH NATURE AS A PARTNER

From walls to gardens to rooftops to windows, the way we build and inhabit our homes is becoming increasingly entwined with nature.

For as long as we have been building, humans have sought to integrate nature with the places we live, whether with views of the outside world or by bringing plants, flowers, and other nonhuman life inside. Now, with global climates changing, the importance of incorporating nature into architecture is more pressing than ever.

A wide variety of techniques

As this book explores, architects around the globe are finding ways of intertwining the natural world with the designed world for both spectacular aesthetic benefits and functional ones, such as for cooling or improving well-being. Many of these designers draw on ideas of biophilia, as Victoria Jackson and Rosa Isaacs of Oliver Heath Design explore in their essay (see p.126) about the human longing for connection with the natural world.

However, while turning the pages of this book, readers will quickly see that there is not one approach to incorporating nature into design. Indeed, the homes and offices contained within this book showcase the wide variety of techniques being used by conscientious architects from Melbourne to Mexico City who design with nature. More than simply technological solutions, however, these projects represent new strains in design that incorporate nature into the heart of architecture with awe-inspiring results.

It all depends on the context

They also show that this future will be as diverse and divergent as the people who design it. Bunkeren, for example, a family home in southwestern Australia designed by James Stockwell, exemplifies a light-touch approach that allows the preexisting natural landscape to roll through mostly untouched (see p. 210). We see this again in Monterrey, Mexico, where Tatiana Bilbao's Los Terrenos house is built around preexisting trees (see p.172), and in Formafatal's Achioté villas, whose rammed-earth structures sit lightly atop the Costa Rican jungle (see p.196).

In urban contexts, other methods are employed by architects seeking to bring a touch of green to the cityscape. The striking Urban Farming Office and Tony Fruit Office, both in Ho Chi Minh City, Vietnam, deploy extensive planting on their facades to shade the building and cool down its surroundings (see pp. 102 and 112). We see similar methods employed in São Paulo and Singapore: the former, a renovation of a midcentury apartment that combines an automated irrigation system with indoor fruit and vegetable plants (see p. 156); the latter, a green oasis in the center of the city-state (see p. 106). Another example, Green House in London, features bamboo planting on its facade, in a reference to the site's history as a greenhouse (see p. 64). In each instance, the presence of greenery and planting provide numerous benefits including air purifying, cooling, shading, and, of course, brightening the days of those living and working in the buildings.

Blurring boundaries

Elsewhere in the book we come across numerous instances of nature entering the realm of the domestic, blurring the boundaries between interior and exterior and challenging what we expect from the home. Few are more striking than Hourré, a renovated farmhouse in the French countryside that features large voids, remnants of the house's former ruinous state, which create unexpected connections between rooms and make large terraces out of former indoor spaces (see p. 164). Most surprisingly, a bathtub sits outside on a landing exposed to the elements. Similarly, Carlo Ratti's creation, The Greenary, is built around a 33-foot (10-meter) ficus tree (see p. 132), while projects in Indonesia feature flourishing internal gardens, complete with the graceful presence of palm trees (see pp. 144 and 150).

A brighter future

Among these spectacular examples are quieter, sensitive, and smart projects employing low-energy technologies for heating and cooling that save natural resources—off-grid projects in Brazil and Mexico collect rainwater, for example (see pp. 38 and 178). Aquas Perma Solar Firma, a domestic renovation in Sydney, features a solar power system for hot water and an irrigation system for a vegetable garden also supplied by rainwater (see p. 42). Considered together, this collection of exceptional architecture

6

forms an argument for the importance of nature in architecture for the well-being of the planet and its diverse inhabitants, encompassing both human and nonhuman species. They give us a sense of a brighter, flourishing future in which architecture is inseparable from the natural world.

—George Kafka

NATURE AND BEYOND

How can we build with
nature? Designers have been
asking this question for the
past 150 years but often
without understanding the
meaning of the word "with."

Think of the great Victorian planner Ebenezer Howard,
who believed that nature could cure the ills of city
life—pollution, disease, and overcrowding. In 1898,
he laid out his vision for a "Garden City," where even
the poorest worker could enjoy green spaces, which
were painfully unavailable in his London.

Today, variants of Howard's "Garden City" have
bloomed across the world but by another name: the
suburb. Suburban areas might exhibit a semblance

of greenery, but it tends to be merely superficial in nature. Their key feature, the lawn, must be carefully mowed, weeded, and watered to imitate an English country estate. Even worse: the creation of "natural" suburbs often destroyed vast swaths of actual nature. Despite their good intentions, Howard and his followers did not build *with* nature; they used it as a prop.

Building with nature means listening to it. In the age of climate change, we cannot afford to simply use green elements for our enjoyment. If we do not build with nature, we will demolish ourselves along with it. This requires more than decorative greenery; our task as designers is much deeper, almost philosophical. It involves ending the conflict between the built and natural environment. In other words, building *with* nature means that architects must take nature as a partner—not an easy feat for a profession where egocentricity often prevails!

First, we must protect nature—and copy nature—in our use of resources. Reducing unnecessary, wasteful building is an even more important strategy, but we still need to create new homes and businesses, especially where the population is growing. When we do have to build, we need to shift away from a linear economy in which resources are used and disposed of in a one-way, straight line. Instead, we need a circular economy, where everything is recycled and reused. When a plant or an animal dies, its body returns to the soil. Could our buildings do the same?

One solution to achieve a circular economy is to embrace natural construction materials. Wood, stone, and mud bricks create much less waste than concrete and steel. Even better, we can use new technologies to create experimental bio-based materials. We can build with mushroom mycelium, or even food waste—and innovate design along the way.

Second, we must bring living things into the built environment—not solely for aesthetic appeal but for practical functionality as well. In *Urban Jungle* (2023), Ben Wilson explains that metropolitan areas are havens of biodiversity. Almost half of Australia's endangered animals live in cities—with lots of trash to eat and alleys to hide in. The biologist E. O. Wilson famously theorized that all humans experience a love of nature called "biophilia." To satisfy that, we need more than fancy parks. Our cities need wild gardens and green corridors for animal migration—more messy but more natural. The more species we save, the more we can help the Earth adapt to climate change. It is perfectly possible to build with nature in the middle of our cities.

Other benefits of green building are even more immediate. Cities from 16th-century Tenochtitlan to 19th-century New York once grew huge amounts of food. We should bring back urban agriculture today. Even if the food produced through urban farming is not enough to feed all city inhabitants, it can foster a closer connection between people and nature. Methods like hydroponics (growing plants in water), aeroponics (growing plants in the air), and robot-assisted indoor farming can help us grow plants in new places, and old-fashioned community gardens can create social opportunities.

This book contains many examples of projects that strive to break down the wall between the natural and artificial. Collectif Encore found an abandoned French farmhouse with a caved-in roof, sunlight pouring in. When they renovated the building, they preserved the hole in the ceiling to honor the structure's natural decay. Across the ocean in Mexico, Javier Senosiain and HW Studio Arquitectos experimented with semiunderground structures that use the earth as a ceiling. The studio Vo Trong Nghia Architects turned its own office into a farm.

All of these projects are steps toward a broader evolution—or revolution—toward reuniting the natural and artificial worlds. There are many fancy names and theories: philosopher Bruno Latour calls it "transhumanism;" anthropologist Albena Yaneva and architect Alejandro Zaera-Polo call it "cosmopolitics." The architect R. Buckminster Fuller famously told us to imagine that we are all passengers on a single "Spaceship Earth" flying across the stars. If we don't protect our environment, the spaceship will fail. Much of the 20th century was defined by an "International Style" of simple glass-and-concrete buildings that all looked alike. The 21st century could be defined by a "Sustainable Style," except that it should not be just a style, but a deeper mission.

Western philosophers also have to learn from cultures they have oppressed and ignored. For millennia, Indigenous peoples around the globe have maintained a close relationship with their land, practicing sustainable ways of life and protecting their environments. For example, First Nations Australians learned to manage the bush with controlled burns; so did Native Americans in California. Our ecological ambitions are not utopian dreams—much has been done before.

To make environmentalism work in design, we must embrace today's tools: the digital revolution. We sometimes think that technology is the opposite of nature, but this dualism misses the point. In fact, sensors, networks, and artificial intelligence can make our buildings more like living things: able to respond and evolve. "Smart" and "sustainable" can form a harmonious alliance.

Nature always finds places to grow: in holes between bricks and cracks in the sidewalk. With technology, we can create new cracks for life to take hold. For example, my design studio has been working on a 51-story "farmscraper" in Southern China, where 108,000 square feet (10,000 square meters) of crops will grow along the walls. Not only will the tower produce enough vegetables to feed 40,000 people a year, but the plants will absorb sunlight and keep the building cool without using air-conditioning.

We do not know which of the above approaches will succeed and which will fail. Natural evolution relies on natural selection. Similarly, in the built environment, we need diverse experiments to discover what works best. Then, if we succeed at changing our way of building, we can change our way of thinking about the natural world. When we see nature as a resource to be exploited or even a purity to keep unblemished, we do it a great disservice by forgetting how much we are part of it. Only by building *with* nature can we remember that we are building and living in nature.

In the words of the Pulitzer-Prize-winning poet Gary Snyder, "Nature is not a place to visit, it is home."

—Carlo Ratti

A tight plot becomes an expansive family home through smart design and space for organic life to flourish.

GARDEN TOWER HOUSE

Garden Tower House is a renovation on a tight plot in Cremorne, a suburb southeast of Melbourne's central business district. Despite the density of the site, the family home has a breezy feel partly facilitated by the perforated breezeblocks that define the site's outer edges. As well as defining the rectilinear forms that sprout up at the back of the plot—the towers—the breezeblocks allow Melbourne's cool light to flow into the building's interior.

From the front door, however, these cuboids are only glimpsed. Instead, visitors are met with a weatherboarded porch and a white picket fence: original features that root the building firmly within the neighborhood. This single-story structure contains two bedrooms and leads into the contemporary additions that contain living spaces, courtyard gardens, an additional bedroom, and a tower-top terrace. Pastel greens and sandy browns define the interior spaces that feel airy and spacious thanks to high ceilings and built-in furniture that maximizes floor space despite the narrow nature of the building plot.

No space on the site is wasted. Every inch works hard to support the life of the family making their home in Garden Tower House, including the gaps between the breezeblocks and the wooden structures of the towers, which feature planting that will eventually grow to take over the silhouette of the whole project. The central courtyard is the gravitational center of the ensemble, acting as a focal point from the ground-floor living spaces and from a glass corridor that links the two towers. Relaxed paving and planting are prominent in the garden, which is bathed in daylight yet sheltered in privacy from the surrounding neighborhood.

Garden Tower House's small central courtyard is a serene focal point, blending daylight and privacy with relaxed paving and lush greenery.

GARDEN TOWER HOUSE

A blending of architectural eras hides a secret garden and a happy home at the core of this sensitive Melbourne extension.

Autumn House in Melbourne is designed to resemble a secret garden hidden behind a street-facing wall. The project carefully adds a new layer to a Victorian row house that features a 1980s renovation by architect Mick Jörgensen and, crucially, a mature elm tree in the backyard. Studio Bright's design sympathetically balances the three different architectural eras of the family home.

The 1980s renovation involved reconfiguring the interior of the original structure as well as the addition of a studio, storerooms, and garden buildings around courtyard spaces. Studio Bright inserted a series of curving and angled moves at ground level that holds new living, kitchen, and dining spaces as well as an activity space at the front of the site. A brick perimeter wall wraps around these new additions, appearing as a simple garden wall around the precious elm, while at the back of the site an angled form rises up over the brick base in a mesh-screen wedge.

At the ground level, operable sliding glass doors and expansive windows allow for seamless passing between interior and exterior, as though the courtyard extends into the living spaces. The indoor spaces are finished with wood paneling and off-white terrazzo kitchen fixtures complemented by fall tones that resonate with the name of the family home. Upstairs in the new wedge unit, the views are more protected; a small terrace garden encloses the bedrooms, both of which sit behind screen layers that filter light and create privacy from the neighbors. In time, the planting will take over these screens to act as a green landmark in the neighborhood, further emphasizing the appearance of a secret garden overflowing with organic life.

A brick perimeter wall, the terrazzo kitchen, and new wood paneling wrap around Autumn House's secret garden (opposite) that is dominated by an elm.

20

AUTUMN HOUSE

Privacy in the bedrooms in the new wedge unit is maintained with metallic screens that filter light and, in time, will become covered with greenery.

Through large windows and flowing living rooms, a 17th-century villa provides inspiration for this Japanese courtyard home.

Surrounded by buildings on all sides, Loop Terrace architect Tomohiro Hata sought an opportunity to create a peaceful oasis amid the dense urbanity of Hyogo in southern Japan. The result is a sheltered courtyard that is surrounded by the home structure—the eponymous "loop." The building separates the house from the city outside and creates a dynamic inward-facing environment that plays with the thresholds between inside and outside.

The studio took inspiration from the Katsura Imperial Villa on the outskirts of nearby Kyoto. This 17th-century estate negotiates its own relationship with the outside through large doorways that generously frame the surrounding garden. A similar approach was taken at the Loop Terrace, where large windows, terraces, glass walls, and large open staircases provide ample views into the center of the plot. The building's material palette is clean and simple, with wooden flooring and window frames inside and polished concrete outside to complement and highlight the plants of the courtyard.

While the courtyard may be the building's center of gravity, the looped interior spaces hold their own charm. Its well-proportioned living areas are built across multiple levels and are contained within exquisite exposed wooden structural detailing. The large windows provide excellent natural lighting and occasionally dramatic shadows are cast through the greenery of the courtyard. The spaces connect to each other via walkways and small staircases. This gives the home a free-flowing energy, such that moving through the spaces involves moving freely between interior and exterior, akin to traversing the canopy of a forest or a hilly landscape.

Tomohiro Hata's Loop Terrace features a tranquil central courtyard, a quiet escape from the dense urbanity of Hyogo in southern Japan.

LOOP TERRACE

A free-flowing garden sits at the heart
of this Belgian home, where even the indoor
spaces have an outdoor feel.

BRAZILIAN RAINFOREST

What makes the heart of a home? In Brazilian Rainforest, a house in Antwerp designed by Bart & Pieter, the garden sits at the center and can be viewed through every one of the house's windows. Not only is it always visible, but it's designed to always be beautiful with evergreen plants, a mossy hill, grass, and rare flowers.

The designers sought to avoid a typical garden with straight lines and concrete planters, opting for a different approach. The combination of exotic plants and flowers, such as kangaroo paws and knotweed, make it feel lush and alive, at times deliberately interfering with the interior life of the couple who lives there. Indeed, the designers aimed to blur the lines between inside and outside. This was achieved by allowing indoor painted walls to flow seamlessly to the outside, as well as the inclusion of a dramatic dragon tree that grows out of the concrete floor in the kitchen. Other techniques for emphasizing the connection between indoors and outdoors include consistency of floor levels and floor-to-ceiling sliding glass doors, which, when slid aside, remove any barrier to the outside. Elsewhere in the project, skylights flood the indoor spaces with daylight that reflects off yellow walls and sturdy exposed brickwork.

Painted walls, floor-to-ceiling sliding glass doors, and a consistent floor line facilitate the blurring of inside and outside in Brazilian Rainforest in Antwerp.

A glass bridge runs through the heart
of this thoughtful renovation that cherishes
the preexisting alongside the new.

FITZROY BRIDGE HOUSE

Often the most sustainable architectural intervention is to work with what's already there. Fitzroy Bridge House in a suburb of Melbourne combines a careful sense of heritage with intelligent ecological design. This conversion of a Victorian-era row house to a design by Matt Gibson Architecture + Design consists of three two-story buildings connected by walkways and a stunning courtyard, all reminiscent of the Mews housing typology.

At the front end of the project, the original facade has been preserved and restored. Here, a welcoming front door leads into living spaces with high ceilings and cornicing that reveal the age of the original home. Moving further back into the plot, however, the contemporary additions, such as curved windows, modern stair details, and exposed wooden finishes, assert themselves with clarity.

Most striking is the addition of a glass-floored bridge that runs between the two ends of the terraced plot, creating a connection between the past and present. Beneath the bridge, a quiet courtyard is flooded with light to support a minimalist garden and pond, a peaceful retreat at the center of a young family home.

At the back end of the plot, salvaged white bricks undulate like suburban hills to form two modern "pavilions." The reuse of the bricks is a smart ecological move that allows the home to harmonize with the local area. In addition to the reused bricks, Matt Gibson's design employs several other environmental strategies including water collection tanks, cross-ventilation, and highly insulated walls and ceilings.

Three two-story units are connected by walkways and a courtyard with a minimalist garden and pond in this conversion of a Victorian-era row house.

A glass-floored bridge (below) runs between the two ends of the plot, creating a connection between the original structure and the new additions.

FITZROY BRIDGE HOUSE

Vines and clever natural design create a sheltered and breezy Amazonian microclimate on a tiny tropical site.

Hidden behind a facade of hit-and-miss brickwork, this office and poolside garden provide a cool shelter from the tropical heat of Manaus in northwestern Brazil. The brainchild of local Laurent Troost Architectures, Tropical Shed uses a variety of low- and high-tech solutions to create a sustainable and welcoming environment. Entering through the doorway beside the perforated facade that allows breezes into the site, visitors are faced with a narrow but deep footprint containing an outdoor meeting space, swimming pool, and enclosed office. Wrapping around these spaces are two double-height "walls" and a "roof," defined by smooth rebars that support different plant species.

Abundant greenery creates the ghostly silhouette of an industrial shed that is cast in vines rather than steel or plastic, and creates shade for an airy internal microclimate. Planted at the base of the walls are PANCs (*Plantas alimentícias não convencionais*)—unconventional edible plants, such as wild ginger and arrowroot, that are increasingly popular in Brazil and can be grown with minimal care.

In addition to the low-tech approach of the cooling plants and cross-breeze from the open facades, the roof of the enclosed office features an automated irrigation system that throws collected rainwater over the tiled roof to physically cool the space. There isn't a gutter, so the roof allows the water to fall into the plant beds, both watering them and psychologically refreshing visitors with the sound of falling water.

The office at the back of the plot (right) features a double-height ceiling and perforated walls for ventilation. The narrow courtyard (opposite) contains an outdoor meeting space and a swimming pool.

TROPICAL SHED

High-tech systems and a chicken coop are at home in this sustainable row house renovation in Sydney.

CplusC Architectural Workshop was approached by the owners of an existing row house in an urban area of Sydney to help them realize their vision of a home that would embody their commitment to the environment. The result is Aquas Perma Solar Firma, a home with a small footprint that aims to reinterpret the row house typology with an in-depth focus on low energy usage alongside other environmentally conscious touches.

One of the key architectural decisions made by the studio was to move vertical circulation—a striking spiral staircase—to the front of the house, freeing up the floor plan for a central courtyard. The courtyard both bathes the interior with Sydey's natural light and adds to the green spaces otherwise provided by a garden filled with planting beds. Together, the greenery provides both vegetables and clean air for the residents. In addition to the outdoor spaces, the house includes an aquaponics system for fish harvesting, rainwater storage for use throughout the home, a wicking bed to filter water, compost, a worm farm, and a chicken coop. The building operates with extremely low carbon emissions and energy consumption, thanks to a 1.5-kW solar PV system, solar hot water, and a rainwater harvesting system that supplies the toilets, laundry, and irrigation.

The material palette of the interior combines an exposed brick wall running along one side of the property with warm wooden structural elements, flooring, and detailing. The centerpiece of the interior is a custom-made adjustable table that allows the living space to transform flexibly between uses. A large bench overarches three smaller tables with adjustable legs to form a place for sitting, eating, standing, chatting, and working.

A chicken coop is housed in the garden of the home alongside a worm farm, an aquaponics system for fish harvesting, and other facilities for biodiversity.

A central courtyard (below) floods the row house in an urban area of Sydney with light and adds more green space to the property.

AQUA PERMA SOLAR FIRMA

Massive volumes blur inside and outside in this warehouse home inspired by geological forms and outdoor living.

ZZ Top House confounds domestic expectations. The design of the house, by CplusC Architectural Workshop, takes its inspiration from the natural forms of geodes: rocks that contain hollow cavities lined with jagged crystals to create dazzling inner worlds. In the same vein, the front of the house reveals little of the unusual spaces held within.

The house is a four-bedroom home, with a massive kitchen and dining area taking up most of its ground floor. A pair of sunken living rooms are a highlight, characterized by a double-height ceiling that echoes the former warehouse that occupied the site. While one of the living rooms is firmly "inside," with a closeable door, the other is exposed to the exterior. The outer living room features a grill, playing with the idea of fully living outside. Floor-to-ceiling windows emphasize the volume of these rooms, while hanging plants hint at the transition from inside to outside. Natural light pours into these rooms from skylights and enormous openings that defy conventional understanding of interior and exterior. The living rooms flow seamlessly into a generous garden filled with plants and rustic elements—reused brick paving, a corten steel fire pit, and custom-made rough wooden furniture.

In keeping with CplusC's other projects, the ZZ Top House features integrated sustainability features. These include cross-ventilation, vital for cooling the house in Sydney's hot summers, and the optimization of thermal mass alongside other solar strategies. Embodied carbon has also been considered in material choices for the house. It includes recycled floorboards and dry-pressed bricks, meaning heritage features are simply restored rather than replaced. In addition, the house features a 10-kW solar system.

Enormous living spaces with double-height ceilings recall the warehouse history of the ZZ Top House site. Natural light pours into these rooms from skylights and vast openings.

Living rooms flow seamlessly into a generous garden (below) filled with plants, rustic elements, and custom-made furniture.

Clean geometry
and careful structural
detailing create a
sun-bathed interior in
this Brazilian home,
an oasis in the big city.

COBOGÓ HOUSE

Cobogó House is defined by the rectilinear geometry of its structure and the interplay between its finely designed interior and exterior spaces. Located in the center of the city of São Carlos, in the Brazilian state of São Paulo, this residential project faces in on itself to prioritize privacy and allow courtyards to serve as living rooms.

Landscaping plays a crucial role in the arrangement of the house, shaping spaces, composing backgrounds, and controlling temperature and solar lighting for its residents. A tree-lined garden allows mottled sunlight into the kitchen and outdoor eating area. The relationship between other spaces on the ground floor is organized by the careful positioning of openings and varying permeability achieved with both built and planted solutions. A garage and office are independent from the rest of the residence and are on the edge of the front facade, maintaining direct visual contact with the street through a metal clapboard.

A single generous room brings the entire common living area together on the ground floor. On the upper floor, where bedrooms and bathrooms are located, the same logic of visual filtering is maintained, in this case with private balconies or garden slabs for common use. The clear visual connections between different parts of the house are facilitated by the structural and material choices of CHX Arquitetos: cast concrete elements give the building a lightness and allow for large openings to bring in natural light and a sense of openness for the house's residents.

The ground floor of the two-story family home consists of one large living area dotted with sunlight from a richly planted, tree-lined garden.

Cobogó House in the center of São Carlos is defined by the geometry of its structure and the interplay between its interior and exterior spaces.

Interlocking volumes support a stunning
fruit garden atop this home built from locally
sourced materials.

THANG HOUSE

The fruit garden flourishing on the roof terrace at Thang House is a breath of fresh air atop the coastal cityscape of Da Nang, Vietnam. Despite its urban context, the house was inspired by an imagined country house full of rich tropical greenery, grasslands, and fresh air dreamed up by VTN Architects's client when he was a child. While not set in the countryside, Thang House is equally dreamy, with its collection of cubed volumes that enframe living, sleeping, and dining spaces across internal and external environments.

The design of the house is best understood as two parallel lines: one for the garden that forms a huge green wall and the other for the living spaces, whose windows and doors face the green wall, bringing natural light, fresh air, and the aromas of grass and flowers to every corner of the house.

The house itself comprises four main boxes, three of which nest inside the largest one. Some of them protrude over the garden and swimming pool. The largest box is covered with gray stone, sourced locally from the Hoa Son rockery mine. The small ones are clad in white brick, again sourced locally from neighboring Quảng Nam province. Narrow gaps in the rooves of the boxes allow for the subtle entry of natural light that reinforces connections between the home's three stories.

To allow the house to operate as sustainably and economically as possible, an automatic watering system recycles and circulates water from a fish pond to the roof garden and back down. In addition, a solar water heating system installed on the roof terrace produces enough energy for the home and its family of occupants.

At Thang House by VTN Architects, an automatic watering system recycles and circulates water from a fish pond to the roof garden and back down.

Low-carbon materials and greenhouse details allow this family home in London to play on its green history.

The Green House lives up to its name with ecological approaches to architecture that honor the orchard and greenhouse history of its site. Located in a quiet residential neighborhood of North London, the house is designed to "re-green" the historically verdant character of the area with ecologically minded materials, low-energy operational solutions, and the seamless integration of nature into the home's design.

Built for a family of five, the Green House sits between two gardens and has an open atrium at its center that brings daylight into the core of the house. Not only does this flood the living area with natural light, but it also assists in cooling the house. The structure is made of cross-laminated timber, a low-carbon material that is left exposed to give the Green House both a natural feel and a small environmental footprint by eliminating the need for dressings and linings.

Moving out to the facades, sliding polycarbonate screens accompany planted bamboo to create shade and give the house a natural flourish. When glimpsed from the outside, the home immediately echoes the former greenhouse on the site with foliage that ripples through the translucent screens. Back at the core of the home, where the double-height living room allows for large plant life to thrive, a steel staircase rises and wraps around the atrium, bringing with it a flash of color. Needless to say, it's green.

The Green House has an open atrium at its center that brings daylight into the core of the building and also assists in cooling the house.

66

GREEN HOUSE

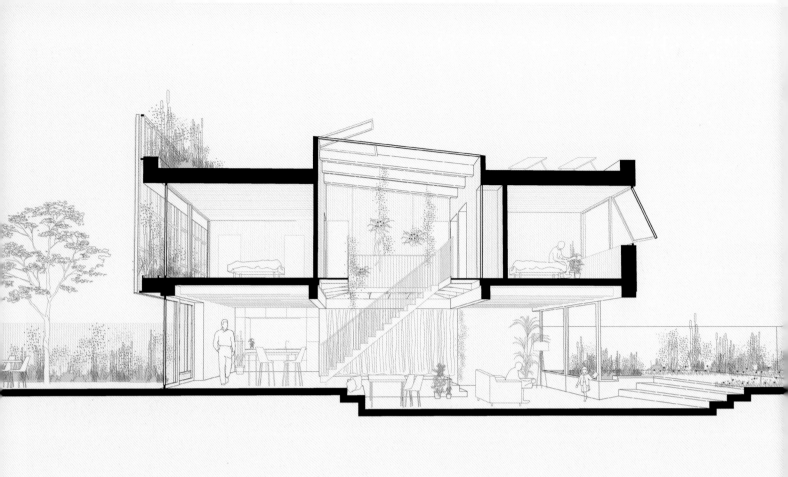

The structure of the home echoes the greenhouses that previously stood on its site in a North London neighborhood.

Clean cuts and
green additions
define the renovation
of this modern family
home in the center
of Mexico City.

CASA VERNE

Nestled in the quiet courtyard of the luxurious Mexico City neighborhood of Polanco, Casa Verne is a 1930s townhouse that has been renovated into a modern family home. The house has a simple footprint and comfortably bears the marks of both the original building and its classy, nature-focused additions.

The house is organized across three stories, each with a distinct character and function. Service spaces occupy the ground floor behind a simple but welcoming foyer characterized by red stone floors and black skirting. Family life takes place on the second story, with a series of parquet floor rooms and picture windows providing generous natural light. Finally, the rooftop garden is a space for privacy amid thriving plant life. Here, floor-to-ceiling sliding glass doors open up panoramic views across the rich greenery toward the rest of Mexico City, giving the impression of a secluded oasis within the buzzing city center.

Key architectural renovations by the Berlin-based architects Zeller & Moye included removing excessive internal walls to create generous living spaces and cutting patios and openings for skylights to maximize daylight in the previously dimly lit lower levels. The rooftop garden was achieved by adding a new floor with a large overhanging roof made of white concrete. Concrete was also used for a bench and table cast into a niche within the garden. Other additions were completed in white marble concrete to achieve a contemporary environment with a fresh character, and the entire floor of the roof features marble pebbles. These are a nod to Mexico City's lost river beds and lakes that formed the landscape before the city was established.

The contemporary rooftop garden of Casa Verne is a space for thriving plant life and privacy amid the hubbub of the Polanco neighborhood.

This Madrid home unfolds across multiple gardens, greenhouses, and courtyards buried beneath an explosion of expressive high-tech architecture.

Tobogán House (TB_House) is located in Aravaca, a residential area on the outskirts of Madrid that straddles the city's urban density and the neighboring El Pardo Woodlands, an ecological and biological reserve. This context informs the design of the house, which blends into its landscape while serving as a spectacular home. Built across three cylindrical stories, the basement and first floor feature gardens and courtyard-like living spaces that merge with the outdoors, where different species of tropical plants thrive.

The landscaping of TB_House combines a mixture of open and more private gardens. Different wild granite rocks were placed between a series of plantings that mix perennials and grasses. There is an earthy path to access the house and small pedestrian paths embedded in the landscape, as well as local pebble gravel and wooden sleepers. More than 50 plant varieties were used, providing color, texture, and movement in the garden, as well as attracting many insects in spring and summer. The private gardens are more sheltered—grassy personal spaces for the resident family's daily life. All the gardens include plants adapted to Madrid's climate, which is characterized by temperatures that fluctuate dramatically between winter and summer. The fluidity of the gardens contrasts with the expressive high-tech nature of the house architecture, where steel beams and trusses are displayed proudly amid the rocky landscape.

The high-tech architecture expressed through steel beams and trusses (right) is on proud display at TB_House, which blends into its landscape.

This Dutch garden is
designed to flourish in
every season, creating
a wild landscape for
its residents to explore.

NATURAL POND GARDEN WITH MODERN CANOPY

This contemporary garden is an enclosed oasis that features spacious terraces and a sturdy canopy with an outdoor kitchen as well as locally sourced plants and winding paths to explore. It was designed with a combination of logical choices and creative flourishes. To create privacy for and from neighboring homes, existing mature pine trees were moved which, alongside evergreen yew clouds and a pole wall, ensure privacy throughout the year.

The garden sits between a house and an outdoor pavilion—these two poles separated by sensitively planted landscaping. The pavilion features an outdoor terrace that was placed behind a natural pond at the center of the garden and oriented to ensure maximum sunlight during long summer evenings. The terrace beneath the canopy is reached following a meandering walkway that also features a break spot with chairs and more hidden routes through the planting. Once at the terrace, visitors enjoy a seating area and an outdoor kitchen. The structure of the pavilion is characterized by metal beams and wooden finishes, giving it a rectilinear solidity amid the overflowing foliage of the garden.

The pond itself is also a luscious green, with leaves and grasses emerging from its still surface. What's more, the surrounding planted nature, including dogwood and larch, reflects off the surface of the pond, creating a multisensory experience that changes with the seasons.

The metal beams and wooden finishes of the pavilion contrast with the overflowing foliage of the garden that reflects off the surface of the pond.

MODERN ARCHITECTURE EMBODIES GREEN SOLUTIONS—INSIDE AND OUT

For countless generations, humans have lived in environments dominated by plants.

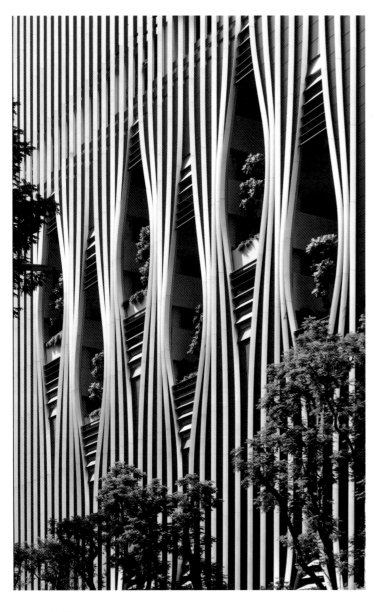

As a result, our eyes have evolved to recognize more shades of green than any other color. Surrounding ourselves with all things green can relieve anxiety and help us feel calm. Studies have also shown that we have a subconscious preference for the complex and organic patterns found in nature. It is no wonder, then, that we are naturally drawn to plants and seek to incorporate them in our day-to-day lives.

Today, many of our spaces, from houses and apartments to offices and shops, are devoid of plants. This absence of plant life can have negative mental and physical effects. Sick Building Syndrome is a term used to describe adverse health symptoms experienced when spending long hours inside, particularly in office buildings. The symptoms are broad and not easily attributed to any one cause, however, poor air quality and atmospheric pollution are thought to be contributing factors. A similar ailment, called Nature Deficit Disorder, attributes negative mental health effects to insufficient time spent in nature. By incorporating planting into our architecture and interior design, we can alleviate such problems, providing easy access to green, visually complex environments that not only improve air quality but also our health and quality of life.

The benefits of using plants in our environment

Plants benefit us in many ways. They convert the carbon dioxide we breathe out into the oxygen we breathe in. Plants can also remove potentially harmful pollution from our air. For example, silver birch trees trap harmful pollutants in their bark, which they then shed. In warmer climates, mangoes and broad-leaved figs have also demonstrated pollution-mitigating properties. Trees are also particularly good at sequestering carbon from the atmosphere into their tissues and locking it away for many years.

The pollution-controlling benefits of plants can also be employed inside where air quality is often poorer. Plant species such as the peace lily, snake plant, and florist's chrysanthemum have all been shown to reduce the amount of pollutants from indoor air. Species such as the spider plant and devil's ivy are particularly well known for their pollution-reducing qualities and have been identified by NASA as plants that effectively reduce air pollution. However, for these effects to be truly beneficial, planting should be abundant. Creative architectural designs such as interior green walls can provide space for ample planting. In addition to improving air quality, plants can also contribute to a building's efficiency. Green roofs reduce energy use because they act as insulators for buildings. They also filter rainwater and reduce flash flooding by slowing the rate at which rainwater reaches the drainage system. Green roofs also have sound-insulating properties that can reduce noise pollution caused by airplanes, cars, and other city noise.

Gardens also play a role in improving our environment by reducing flooding and the energy required to cool our homes. Vegetated gardens allow rainwater to drain away mitigating flood risk. Trees increase this effect by penetrating deeper soil with their roots. They also improve the thermal efficiency of buildings during summer with their shade. In warmer climates, this can decrease the reliance on air-conditioning, consequently lowering the building's energy usage and costs.

Use of plants in architecture and interior design

So what's the best way to incorporate planting into interior and exterior architectural design? These two environments are often vastly different, and careful consideration should be given to choosing the best solution that suits the individual project. Green facades, green roofs, gardens, green walls, and interior landscaping, especially when used in combination, can dramatically transform a space, improving its appearance and ambiance.

Exterior green solutions

Green facades are changing the face of exterior architectural design. Not only do they keep buildings cool but they also clean the air. One common method of creating a green facade involves planting climbing plants, such as Boston ivy, English ivy, or climbing hydrangea, at the base of the wall and encouraging them to climb up the facade. Another method involves using a proprietary green wall solution that has individual plant cells connected within a frame

that includes an integrated watering system. Intricate patterns and effects can be created by varying the mix and variety of plants used in green facades.

Green roofs top many modern designs and are becoming more prevalent in both residential and commercial design. They fall into two broad categories—intensive and extensive. Intensive green roofs or roof gardens are accessible and have deeper rooting zones to accommodate larger plants, trees, and shrubs. They can only be installed on buildings designed to withstand the additional weight of larger plant life and foot traffic. Extensive green roofs typically have shallow rooting substrates that can only support lower-growing plants such as grasses as well as other herbaceous plants. They are lightweight and suitable for small structures like garages and sheds as well as larger buildings like offices and apartments. They can also be retrofitted to existing roofs. The load-bearing capacity of the building is the main determining factor when considering what type of green roof is right for the building.

Of course, the humble garden should not be overlooked as an important design element in any architectural scheme. Gardens increase extra living space for cooking, dining, socializing, and relaxing outdoors. As extensions of the living spaces, gardens (as well as courtyards and terraces) can also greatly increase the value of a home. Research has also shown that gardening is good for our physical and mental health, improving both physical fitness and mood.

Solutions for increasing planting indoors

The right planting can also improve indoor spaces, no matter how small. However, there are several important factors to consider. The indoor climate is often very different from the outside. Light levels can be hundreds of times lower inside and it is usually less humid than outside. Finally, indoor temperatures are usually warmer than the outside climate in winter and cooler in the summer.

Despite these differences, green walls offer a relatively easy way of incorporating a large amount of planting into a small space. There are many readily available hydroponic green wall solutions where the plants grow in water containing plant nutrients.

These systems are often low maintenance and can be cared for by horticultural contractors. Integrated LED lighting systems allow green walls to be installed in areas with low natural light levels.

Interior landscaping is another green solution that encompasses a range of approaches and techniques, some on a grand scale. The choice of plants is limited to those from tropical or subtropical climates with a similar temperature range to our preferred indoor climate. In larger spaces, a more natural-looking, layered effect can be achieved with low-growing groundcover plants, shrubs, and larger species like figs and fan palms that create dramatic effects with their impressive heights.

Plants can be incorporated into any interior space that has enough light and someone to maintain them. Stunning effects can be achieved, even on a limited budget, by varying plant shapes, textures, colors, and heights. Individually potted plants offer great flexibility because the designer is not limited to choosing plants that require similar amounts of water. For example, a taller dracaena that prefers drier soil can be paired with a low-growing baby's tears, which tolerates more moisture.

Plant choice considerations

Of course, not every plant can thrive in every environment, and the choice can be quite overwhelming for those who want to go green. For best results, consider the eventual height and form of the plant, its preferred climate, and its maintenance requirements. When choosing a plant for a green facade or green wall, go with herbaceous plants that don't grow very tall. Species such as bamburata and the smaller bromeliads have a lower habit and would be equally at home in a green wall indoors or a green facade in tropical climates. However, neither species would survive outdoors in northern Europe or North America. Some species can be used in specific circumstances with the correct maintenance. For example, Himalayan birch grows in mountainous regions reaching heights of 50 feet (15 meters) in the wild. Employing a pruning technique known as copicing can restrict their growth, making them suitable for utilization in roof gardens.

Plant life greatly enhances our living spaces—both inside and out. No longer just green decoration, plants and landscapes now take center stage in contemporary architectural design, as the innovative projects within these pages exemplify. Such informed design demonstrates that by listening to and learning from nature, it is possible to create lush and verdant environments teeming with the health benefits and added well-being that only plant life can create.

—Ashley D. Penn

Steel stepping stones bounce through the center of this garden transformation, an ode to the rhythms of the natural world.

This garden in Eindhoven has a poetic and symbolic design, which interprets Japanese landscaping in a European context. A bridge from the project's main house signals the departure from the familiar world toward nature and a sanctuary for meditation in the form of a teahouse. The teahouse features a seating area and a fireplace beneath a roof of exposed wooden beams held up by bamboo columns. By following meandering paths around the garden, visitors not only experience the green space from its multiple rewarding perspectives, but also enter a mindful and immersive headspace. As the garden continues, the house seems to fade from view, and the shade of the absorbing nature takes over.

The materiality of the garden is informed by *wabi-sabi* principles that allow the garden to exist in an imperfect state, always evolving and aging in different ways as the seasons pass. It is the designer's intention that the garden becomes more profound as it ages. Moss will form and soften its edges, for example.

One of the highlights of the garden is its bridge, a series of interconnected 0.8-inch- (2-centimeter-) thick raw steel plates. These plates are placed across the water at the center of the garden like a series of industrial stepping stones or lily pads. In keeping with the tones of the rest of the garden, the bridge will be allowed to rust, aging gracefully with the trees surrounding it. The pond itself is characterized by boulders and light planting, which give the water a cloudy and mysterious feel.

A line of thin steel plates across the water at the center of the garden acts as stepping stones to connect the teahouse with the rest of the garden.

JAPANESE WATER GARDEN

City farming has
a new face at this
buzzing Copenhagen
rooftop, where
fruits, vegetables,
and herbs are
available for citizens
and chefs alike.

Above the hustle and bustle of Copenhagen, organic vegetables of many kinds thrive. ØsterGro is the first rooftop farm in Denmark located in the climate-resilient neighborhood of Østerbro. Lush vegetable gardens, arranged neatly in rows, occupy most of the roof and an adjoining restaurant invites Copenhagenites to get up close and personal with food production.

Located on top of the Nellemannhuset car auction building, ØsterGro covers 6,500 square feet (600 square meters) with fields of organically grown vegetables, fruits, greens, herbs, edible flowers, a greenhouse, henhouse, and even beehives. A narrow paved path brings visitors across the roof, making the gardens accessible and leading the way to the rooftop restaurant. A small greenhouse offers dining experiences at long tables where visitors can enjoy the leafy view.

The project was founded in 2014 by Sofie Brincker, Livia Urban Swart Haaland, and Kristian Skaarup, who grow food according to organic principles. They provide vegetables, honey, and eggs to the members of the farm. When the harvest season begins, members can pick up their share of greens every Wednesday, but ØsterGro is not only for the members and volunteers who participate in the project. It is a green breathing space for the whole city, and allows us to reconsider how rooftops can be used in urban environments and how we think about food production.

A small greenhouse restaurant offers dining experiences at ØsterGro rooftop farm, where visitors can enjoy the leafy view.

97

A multistory housing block in the center of Amsterdam rethinks the role of the green roof in contemporary cityscapes.

Designed to be playful, generous, and light, Groenmarkt is a building for humans, plants, butterflies, birds, and bees that rethinks how green roofs can be used in the city.

The housing block in Amsterdam's city center is designed with its insides facing outward. Rather than a formal facade, it features an irregular and playful frontage that is lushly green and lively. Hidden amid the bricks of its structure are holes for birds to nest, and climbing plants weave their way from the building's base up to its balconies. This continues up onto the building's most spectacular feature: the roof. Here, a surreal dune landscape contains a pool for residents to take a dip.

The roofscape is shaped with the Dutch coast in mind: a little rugged and suited to the breezy northern European climate. It features indigenous plants suitable for harsh, extreme, and windy circumstances, such as pine trees planted in sand and shells that form an ideal substrate for coastal vegetation. Bees, butterflies, and other insects also thrive on the roof alongside the plants. With this project, the architects at Buro Harro wanted to explore how roofs could be a resource for city living and a place for nature to thrive. Typically, roofs are left bare to absorb heat and simply hold infrastructure materials. At Groenmarkt, they show how city roofs can boost biodiversity, create energy, cool the city, capture rain, and create a space for residents and citizens to enjoy.

A rooftop pool (above) is surrounded by a surreal dune landscape for humans and other species to enjoy. It features indigenous plants suitable for extreme, harsh, and windy circumstances.

GROENMARKT

A wall of green erupts across this office, an innovative and radical solution to overheating Vietnamese cities.

Urban Farming Office is a response to the rapid urbanization of Vietnamese cities and the issues associated with this development. Ho Chi Minh City is among those urban centers suffering from heavy traffic, pollution, flooding, and overheating. This project, by VTN Architects, is an attempt to bring green space back to the cityscape. In addition, with its overhanging planters, the building provides space for vertical urban farming, promoting safe food production in the city.

Located on a street corner in a newly developed area of Ho Chi Minh City, Urban Farming Office is an office building, although at first glance it appears more like an overgrown bush. Greenery erupts from every pore of the facade, such that it's almost hard to imagine a building standing behind. The planters descend from the roof via a concrete structure and a series of steel rods. The boxes are easily added and removed, allowing for taller plants to grow comfortably, and are irrigated with collected rainwater. Among the philodendrons and palms, vegetables, herbs, and fruit trees thrive on the facade of the building.

The wall of green also creates a microclimate within the building by sheltering it from city heat, eliminating the need for air-conditioning. The concrete structure is completely exposed across the office building's six stories, with double- and triple-height voids between floors that create a cavernous sense of space. These interconnections between floors also increase the volume of the inhabitable space, balancing the lack of city views outside.

An exterior wall of green protects a cavernous interior microclimate at Urban Farming Office in a newly developed area of Ho Chi Minh City.

URBAN FARMING OFFICE

A tower transforms Singapore's dense
financial district into a lively green oasis
with the city's tallest urban farm.

With over 80,000 plants and a total landscaped area of more than 90,000 square feet (8,300 square meters), the CapitaSpring tower reinforces Singapore's reputation as a garden city. The tower is located at the center of the city state's financial district and features office, retail, and residential spaces spread across its 51 floors and behind an undulating facade that reveals pockets of green amid the dense urban fabric.

At street level, the CapitaSpring tower reinvigorates a historic section of Market Street with a newly pedestrianized public realm. Hefty planters populate a landscaped area that creates new green breathing space in the high-density Central Business District. Stepping into the footprint of the megastructure, a "City Room" creates a shaded entrance to retail, office, and residential lobbies. On the building's second and third floors, 56 food stalls draw in local workers and residents, cementing the location's importance as a social center within the community.

Above eight floors of residential properties, four connected levels of organic softscape form an open-air garden. The planting of this area mimics the plant hierarchy of a tropical rainforest as dictated by the availability of light. Shade-tolerant plants with large leaves are found on the "rainforest floor," requiring the least amount of direct light, while the roof of the "rainforest" features trees defined by their smaller leaf structure. Topping it all is CapitaSpring's rooftop garden, with views of the city over Singapore's tallest urban farm.

CapitaSpring tower's facade undulates to reveal pockets of green amid Singapore's urban fabric (above). Four connected levels of organic softscape form an open-air garden (opposite and left).

At street level, the tower reinvigorates the public space of the Central Business District and underlines Singapore's reputation as a garden city.

SPRING

Amid the heat of Ho Chi Minh City, a green ziggurat office embodies sustainable cooling strategies.

Sitting on a corner plot in Ho Chi Minh's lively District 4, the four-story Tony Fruit Office building receives direct sunlight from dawn until dusk. While this may make for spectacular sunsets and views, it also has the potential to cause serious problems with overheating in interior spaces.

The solution, devised by architects TAA Design, comes in the form of a wooden baton structure affixed to the building's two sun-facing facades, which has three key benefits. Firstly, it acts as a network of brise-soleils, with the wooden batons creating a series of shades that prevent daylight from penetrating the floor plates of the office building. Secondly, the wooden structure provides a platform for extensive planting that surrounds the building; cooling the air, providing yet more shade; and bringing greenery into the urban context. The ziggurat structure allows small trees to punctuate the exterior, creating the sense that the structure has simply grown organically from the street trees below. Finally, the natural tones and rectilinear geometry of the wooden structure give the building a distinctive presence in the streetscape.

This wooden materiality flows smoothly into the interior of the building, with exposed ceiling beams echoing the tones of the exterior structure. Similarly, floor-to-ceiling windows enable uninterrupted views of the planting on the facade, contributing to an enhanced sense of well-being. Yet more than benefitting the day-to-day experience of the workers inside the building, Tony Fruit Office offers a replicable model for dealing with extreme heat that is both natural and sustainable.

The natural tones and rectilinear geometry of Tony Fruit Office's wooden structure give the building a distinctive street presence.

A cavernous hotel is built onto the site of a 300-year-old Japanese guesthouse with a spectacular sunlit atrium of intertwined walkways.

SHIROIYA

HOTEL

Designed by Sou Fujimoto, the Shiroiya Hotel in Maebashi, in central Japan, is a dramatic renovation built into the shell of a preexisting inn, which had welcomed guests for over 300 years. Its lounge space at the atrium's ground level serves as a living room for the city that invites all people, not just guests, in from the street outside to gather. It sits beneath a huge cavity that was carved out of the original building and left open with powerful concrete columns and exposed beams that are dappled with the natural rays that enter from upper-level skylights.

Ascending the atrium toward the guest rooms, visitors have a profound spatial experience as intertwined staircases and structural elements create dynamic views and perspectives, akin to moving through a city. The guest rooms are located on the upper floors, with each one designed by globally famous architects and other designers, including Jasper Morrison, Michele de Lucchi, and Sou Fujimoto himself. An open passageway leads through to an extension of the Heritage Tower on a plot that was previously a terrace over a tributary of the Tone River. The extension is named Green Tower and is covered in a green hill that serves as a new urban space and route through the neighborhood. For Sou Fujimoto Architects, the addition continues some of the key oppositional themes of the project, "such as new/old, outside/inside, and urban/architectural."

The atrium of Shiroiya Hotel is filled with powerfully exposed concrete engineering lit by upper-level skylights and serves as a living room for the city.

SHIROIYA HOTEL

Experiments in domesticity and sustainability define this forest-like home that sprouts out of the Vietnamese soil.

Labri is a pavilion-like home that challenges our assumptions of how architecture can shape the way we live. Located at the end of a small alleyway, the house appears like a secret, with four distinct volumes of steel and glass that erupt out of the central Vietnamese city of Huế and form a cluster of angular shapes topped by frangipani trees.

At first glance, they appear as large-scale sculptures or an organic forest rather than individual rooms for a couple approaching retirement. Yet this is a home, and one that seeks to blend seamlessly with the plants, birds, and other species that are present on the site. Each room is a single story constructed in three layers. A facade of glass forms the outside. Next, a layer of vines creates shade and intertwines nature into the structure of the home. Finally, a layer of concrete provides structural support and flooring for the units inside.

Each of the rooms is encased almost entirely by glass, which means the surrounding plants and rooms are always visible—as is the moon and stars at night. The rooms are connected by pathways, and fixed ladders allow access to their roofs. On top, the residents can relax as if high up in the canopy of a forest, with clear views of the height-restricted historic neighborhood in the center of Huế.

Each glass block has a different function. There is a living/dining room, a kitchen, a bathroom, and a bedroom, all minimally decorated to allow for basic needs. Overall, the Labri house feels like a playful labyrinth; a shelter to be at one with and amid the surrounding nature.

Labri's rooms are connected by pathways (opposite). The bedroom (left) is almost entirely encased in glass, meaning the surrounding plants are always visible.

WHY NATURE? WHY NOW?

You may be asking yourself
what nature has to do with
design and why.

In recent years, there has been so much interest and talk surrounding interior design that draws inspiration from the natural world. The short answer is that nature is the best designer. There is little waste in nature, with every element in dynamic balance within larger ecological systems, providing endless beauty and innovation. This means that learning from nature can help us address design challenges in a joyful way that is also beneficial for the well-being of all.

Today, more than half of the world's population lives in urban settings, but this wasn't always the case. Humans have evolved in rich multisensory environments, and much of what was vital to us in such settings is still significant to us now—evident by the fact that many of us actively seek respite in the great outdoors. Research demonstrates that interactions with nature are beneficial to our well-being. Yet, in our towns and cities, we are often disconnected from any form of nature or natural landscapes. In fact, in Europe and North America, we spend the vast majority of our time inside the buildings and vehicles we have created—unlike our predecessors who spent nearly all of their time outside. This has left many of us disconnected and out of sync with nature; most of the time we can live with our daily lives fairly unaffected by changing weather, cycles of light and dark, and seasons.

Yet research tells us that this disconnection is detrimental not only to our physical and psychological health, but also to the other species with whom we share this planet. As we wake up to the realization that we are an integral part of the living systems on this planet, there is a huge opportunity to learn from nature with respect and humility. After all, the other species and ecological systems around us are the result of millions of years of evolution, each iteration an improvement on the last. So, it should come as no surprise that we humans are now looking to nature to learn how to better design our spaces, as well as our materials, products, and services. But to do this, we need to design them with an understanding that we are a part of nature. Because when we appreciate that we are nature, it changes the way we think about the world around us and we can start to design with nature rather than against it.

Biophilic Design

Imagine what would happen if nature designed our spaces, buildings, and cities. What would they look like? There would certainly be plenty of natural light, fresh air, greenery, and water. How would they feel? Probably like spaces where life could flourish, and well-being is supported. They'd be made from materials in organic forms with a variety of textures, sounds, and smells.

And how would they be arranged? Perhaps the inside of our buildings would feel more like forests with canopies stretching overhead to provide shelter from the weather while allowing enough dappled light and air through for life to thrive within. Other interiors might emulate big open savannahs, offering long sight lines over landscapes made up of diverse colors, patterns, and textures.

Biophilic design draws upon the concept of "biophilia," which means the human desire, or predisposition, to connect with nature. It offers methods for bringing nature into our built environments, helping us ask the question, "How would nature design this?"

There are three core experiences of biophilic design: direct experiences of nature, indirect experiences of nature, and experiences of space and place. An authentic approach to biophilic design aspires to incorporate all three experiences in a well-considered combination.

Direct experiences of nature can be brought in through planting, natural lighting, ventilation, and water features wherever possible. Such elements greatly benefit the well-being of those who use the space and can also support planetary health if selected consciously.

Indirect experiences of nature are often easier to introduce into spaces because they can be brought in through materials, forms, and furniture—either sourced directly or by replicating those found in nature. For example, a rich sensory experience can be created by including or mimicking the patterns, textures, and colors found in different natural landscapes.

Experiences of space and place use nature for inspiration when considering spatial layout—creating shelter, long sight lines, and the sense of mystery you might experience in natural landscapes. If you

contemplate the vast array of biospheres that exist across our beautiful planet, from mountain ranges and shorelines to deserts and rivers, it's no wonder nature offers endless inspiration when it comes to designing spatial experiences.

Biophilic Materials

The principles of biophilic design explain some of our evolutionary preferences for certain materials, while science and innovation offer insights into how materials impact our well-being. Certain materials carry a magnetism—from their color and their tactile qualities to the way they patina and age over time. Materials of natural origin have the dual effect of appealing to our senses while benefiting our health and well-being at the same time.

The practice of interior design is in the midst of a material renaissance. Where mass production distanced us from the origin of materials, a renewed interest in materials that benefit both the planet and people has seen us grow closer to the fabric that makes up our spaces. But are all materials created equal? In short, the answer is no.

You may be thinking all natural materials are good for the environment and people, but what really makes a material "good" is more complex. For example, asbestos is a material derived from natural origins, but we all know by now that it is detrimental to human health.

Within the practice of biophilic design, the focus is on the attributes of the materials that contribute to the well-being of both people and planet. After all, extracting natural materials in a way that is detrimental to nature to create a nature-inspired interior is counterproductive. Whereas selecting materials that are in tune with the natural environment and have known benefits for our well-being is an effective way of working with nature.

Wood, for instance, is regenerative due to its growing process, and benefits our well-being when used in interior spaces—lowering both heart rates and stress levels—and appeals to our tactile and visual senses. When considering the well-being of the planet in wood production, multiple third-party accreditations can ensure it has been sourced responsibly. An incredibly versatile material, wood can be brought into our spaces in multiple ways—from the structure to interior wall treatments such as paneling and slatting, as well as furnishing and fixtures. It's always important to select with an understanding of the local context—a rule that should apply to all materials. By doing so, we ensure that what we bring into a space is ecologically and culturally relevant with both environmental and place-making benefits.

Cork, a material derived from the same source as wood—albeit the dead outer layer that is removed while the tree itself is left to regrow—is another naturally existing material that is making a comeback. Long considered to be a relic from the 1970s and relegated to the task of bottle-stopping, this fascinating material is having a resurgence of interest. This is largely thanks to the progression of cork finishes, which make the material more aesthetically appealing for interiors, adding to its existing sound absorption qualities and tactile appeal.

While no one material is going to be "perfect," it is important to weigh the value a material brings to an interior against the well-being impact it has—on the living species that exist both inside and outside of a space.

The Rise of Well-Being

In recent years, well-being has become a priority for many, and there is now a greater understanding of the benefits of nature for human health. This can be seen around the world in the use of nature's healing powers in healthcare, as well as targets set for architects and designers through building certifications.

Whereas we used to seek nature experiences outside, there is now an increased awareness of the fact that we can benefit from connections to nature wherever we are. As a result, we've started to also usher it into our interiors—which makes sense, as they are where we spend most of our time. While planting and greenery are an important part of doing this in an impactful way, biophilic design considers more than just direct nature touchpoints.

Creating interiors that have both real and expressed nature experiences brings many benefits to

our well-being and spatial encounters. Pair this with an understanding that we must be sensitive about what we take from nature to create these experiences, and we start to also reframe our position within our living systems.

Our understanding of well-being is also evolving. After all, it isn't just the connections to nature—direct or indirect—that support our psychological and physical health, but also our connections to each other. While technology advances and offers more virtual experiences and global connections, there is also a yearning for interactions that create a sense of place and bond us to our communities. Spaces within our buildings that reflect the surrounding culture and ecology can create a beneficial feeling of connectedness and belonging.

Nature is more than just green spaces; it's made up of connected living systems with a diversity of landscapes and species—including us humans. If we want to authentically emulate nature in our spaces, we first need to expand our understanding of it. Biophilic design can help by giving us the tools to create holistic approaches to green interiors while allowing us to better understand how they contribute to our well-being.

—Victoria Jackson & Rosa Isaacs
Oliver Heath Design

An ancient tree forms the core of this farmhouse conversion, a classy home amid the lush landscape of Parma.

THE GREENARY

The Greenary is a private home built around a 33-foot (10-meter) ficus tree. The tree, named Alma, stands in the middle of the house's main living area and thrives in the stable temperatures of the indoor space. This radical move, in the midst of a traditional Italian farmhouse, showcases new approaches to blurring the boundaries between the natural and artificial realms in architecture.

To create the ideal setting for the tree to thrive, Carlo Ratti Architects completely redesigned the preexisting farmhouse to maximize natural light, installing a 33-foot (10-meter) south-facing glass wall. Both the windows and the roof can be opened and closed automatically to adjust the amount of sunlight and fresh air entering the house, controlling the temperature and humidity so that the tree and the home's occupants can live together comfortably. A staircase beside the tree draws the house's residents upward to different floors while retaining close proximity to the house's protagonist, Alma.

Elsewhere in the house, subtle touches allow its occupants to remain connected to the surrounding Parma landscape. Upon arrival, residents and visitors descend a bit to exist at eye level with the idyllic meadow outside and stone floors that incorporate soil. Elsewhere in the complex, a workspace was converted from a granary, and a garden, landscaped by designer Paolo Pejrone, celebrates the biodiversity of the region.

A ficus tree stands at the center of The Greenary's central atrium, reaching to the floors above. A staircase beside the tree hangs down from the ceiling, as if held by vines.

Smart design and sustainable solutions
combine to make this Sydney corner home
a nature-friendly domestic masterpiece.

Standing on a Sydney corner site, Welcome to the Jungle House bursts at its seams with urban greenery. The home of CplusC Architectural Workshop's director Clinton Cole, the three-story house is built within a heritage facade on a triangular-shaped plot, which is separated from the newer structure inside by a narrow cavity. This gap allows abundant light to enter the home while providing privacy and thermal regulation. Galvanized steel planting beds provide the structural bracing between the two skins and are filled with plants that cool the incoming breezes via transpiration.

The home itself needed to be flexible enough for a growing family and sustainable in all aspects—environmentally, socially, and economically. This sustainability has been achieved with a number of explicit technical solutions, as well as more subtle design strategies. For example, the house features a solar-paneled facade, an irrigation system using recycled water, and low-energy LED lighting. Yet more than this, the house is designed with flexible living spaces to adapt to the family's growth without needing significant future renovations, and ensuring the home will last generations without the need for demolition. Similarly, the steel structure, although higher in embodied energy, requires less maintenance and will long outlive the alternative timber structural elements. Finally, the rooftop garden and beehive provide abundant food for the family, who share the excess with friends and neighbors.

The three-story house is built within a heritage facade and has a varied material palette including polished concrete, exposed timber beams, and steel planters.

WELCOME TO THE JUNGLE HOUSE

The rooftop garden and beehive (right) of the Welcome to the Jungle House provide abundant food for the resident family and their neighbors.

WELCOME TO THE JUNGLE HOUSE

142

WELCOME TO THE JUNGLE HOUSE

An indoor tropical garden sits at the heart of this palatial house in Bali, framing stunning views of volcanoes and rice fields.

CALA SAONA

Cala Saona is an oasis in the heart of Canggu in southern Bali, Indonesia, on a plot that faces sunset and is surrounded by stunning rice fields. The house was designed to create a family home flexible enough to host extended relatives coming to visit Bali.

This result is one main house—a five-bedroom structure with en suite bathrooms—as well as a guest pavilion that is located lower in the naturally sloping plot, and itself holds three en suite bedrooms as well as a pool and terrace. The centerpiece of the main house is an indoor tropical garden that sits beneath a cavernous 30-foot (9-meter) roof and surrounds a sunken living area. Palm trees tower above the residents while shorter foliage sprouts between the backs of sofas and the neutral hard floor. The house seems to have been constructed around the palms; in places, the trees sprout straight through the lower ceilings of the complex. Elsewhere, canopies of wicker and straw create shade on the terraces for the house guests.

Mediating the relationship between interior and exterior, the central living area features floor-to-ceiling windows and abundant cross-ventilation to passively deal with the Indonesian heat. The living area flows seamlessly to an outdoor terrace, complete with wood-paneled seating and dining areas with spectacular views of rice fields and nearby volcanoes. Beyond the terrace, a huge swimming pool made from locally sourced marble meanders out from the house, appearing more like the edge of the sea than a home pool.

The palm trees sprout through the floor and ceilings of Cala Saona's indoor tropical garden (opposite), the centerpiece of the main house.

147

The living area flows seamlessly into an outdoor terrace with a huge swimming pool, complete with wood-paneled seating and dining areas.

Natural vegetation is part of the furniture at this vacation house in Bali, where every corner seems to sprout with greenery.

Cala Blanca is a four-bedroom building packed onto a 4,300-square-foot (400-square-meter) Balinese plot that emphasizes connections to nature. Its designers, the Bali-based Biombo Architects, sought to create a biophilic home that would allow natural vegetation to be as welcome as its furniture and guests. Sunken sofa areas are surrounded by palm trees and other plants that nestle in corners, beside walkways, and in raised planters, catching the eye and creating a sense of well-being for the house's residents. Alongside organic elements, natural light and ventilation flood the home and natural materials, such as wood and stone, enhance a sense of environmental connection and comfort.

Stepping into the home, guests are dropped into an open-plan living area beneath a high-sloped wooden ceiling that covers the kitchen, living room, and dining room. High internal windows add to the sense of volume inside the house and allow for the crossing of natural light through different parts of the structure. Connected to the sunken sofa area is a multipurpose room that can be used as an office, playroom, or additional bedroom. A mezzanine bedroom with a secret staircase perches above the kitchen, hidden from sight.

Outside, the home's center of gravity is the striking swimming pool. Designed to emulate a turquoise beach, the pool rests under the shadow of coconut trees and slips fluidly from the turfed landscape to a cool, white stone finish.

Natural materials in the open-plan living area, such as wood and stone, enhance a sense of environmental connection and comfort at Cala Blanca.

CALA BLANCA

Sunken sofa areas are surrounded by
palm trees and other plants (opposite).
A cool white stone finish characterizes
the swimming pool (below) that rests
under Balinese coconut trees.

155

A verdant haven in the urban jungle of
São Paulo, this apartment pairs high-tech
systems with natural solutions.

THE TERRACE APARTMENT

How do you bring nature into a home if the house doesn't have a balcony, terrace, or garden? For the designers of Estudio Guto Requena, the answer was to turn an entire apartment into a terrace. The namesake apartment is a green haven amid the urban jungle of São Paulo, with foliage erupting from every windowsill, shelf, and even the ceiling.

Located close to downtown São Paulo where the gems of Brazilian modernism rub shoulders, the Terrace Apartment is the renovation of a two-bedroom apartment in a 1962 building by Botti and Rubin. The home sits behind a double-skin facade, with layers of geometrically patterned shades and floor-to-ceiling windows that let in ample sunlight to sustain the plant life inside. The apartment is dotted with fruit trees, flowers, and even a productive vegetable garden, making it hard to imagine the presence of the metropolis outside. Much of this greenery is facilitated by a suspended flower box that spans the different living environments contained within.

Rather than separate these environments into distinct rooms, the layout of the apartment is dictated by activities: working, sleeping, eating, socializing, and relaxing. The floor plan is flexible, with moving walls and pieces of furniture, such as a rotating desk, which make the space as dynamic and alive as the vegetation flourishing inside. This energy extends beyond the architecture and spatial planning into the digital realm, with automated systems for lighting, curtains, access, and, most importantly, watering, building upon decades of research into "hybrid dwelling" by Estudio Guto Requena. This thriving habitat not only benefits the well-being of its residents, but it also serves to purify and cool down the air of the home—a vital benefit of supporting nature in major cities.

The floor plan of the renovation of a two–bedroom apartment in a 1962 building is flexible, with moving walls and pieces of furniture.

159

Geometrically patterned shades control the flow of sunlight through the modernist facade to the apartment.

THE TERRACE APARTMENT

The São Paulo home is dotted with fruit trees, flowers, and even a productive vegetable indoor garden. It features automated systems for access, lighting, curtains, and watering its many plants.

163   THE TERRACE APARTMENT

Through perforations, voids, and unexpected twists, this restored farmhouse in France lets the outside in.

HOURRÉ

Nestled in the hills of southwest France's Basque Country, a run-down farmhouse has been sensitively transformed into a thriving ecosystem for both human and nonhuman inhabitants. When Anna and Julien Chavepayre of Collectif Encore first came across the crumbling structure, they found that parts of the roof had caved in, and the surrounding vegetation had begun to root in its walls and floors. The couple decided to let this natural resilience inform their design approach, leaving the house roughly as it was found and making light-touch renovations. The result is a truly unique and playful home where plants thrive, and the expected boundaries of the domestic realm are constantly blurred.

Across Hourré's three floors, covered exterior spaces such as terraces and decks—leftover from the house's dereliction—flow seamlessly into the interior through sliding glass doors. Meanwhile, the rooms inside morph fluidly across voids and perforations to defy typical functional uses—a kitchen sits beside a bedroom, and a bathroom can become a living room. The result is a hive of intermingling activities: a "manifesto for a living house," as the architects put it.

On the upper floors, the presence of the natural world is felt with large skylights that, along with the stone walls, allow for passive heating and cooling. Besides the giant hammocks above the dining room table, the *pièce de résistance* is the open bathroom on Hourré's top floor. Where a caved-in roof might have meant disaster, Collectif Encore saw an opportunity to create an extraordinary space. The open-air bathroom faces the Pyrenees for the most stunning of bathing experiences, again dissolving the separation of the house from its surroundings.

Giant hammocks stretch above the expansive dining room table of the playful home, where dinner is served with views of the Pyrenees.

An open-air bathroom on the upper floor of the house (left) makes for extraordinary bathing experiences.

HOURRÉ

A deconstructed house sits quietly amid the forest of Monterrey, where natural preservation is central to architectural design.

Los Terrenos reconfigures what we understand a house to be, deconstructing it to its most basic elements and spreading them out across its site, nestled in a forest near Monterrey, Mexico. The house, a vacation retreat, comprises two pavilion-like structures with different functions. The largest of the two is the more public facing, with a living room, work area, and kitchen. The smaller, L-shaped block contains bedrooms and bathrooms. The two blocks are separated by a square courtyard, which appears more as a clearing in the forest than a paved insertion.

Materially, the structures are simple, sensitive, and occasionally striking. Clay bricks and rammed earth provide a grounding base material, with black metal profiles and mirrored glass creating accents that stand out amid the sloping wooded landscape of the house. Extensive glass wraps around both structures, highlighting the real protagonist of this scheme: the natural landscape. In the bedroom block, each room faces outward in a different direction, so no two views are the same, and the bedrooms themselves feature retractable glass facades to dissolve the boundary between forest and home.

Continuing this thread, the preexisting trees were maintained and respected during the construction of Los Terrenos. The house was built around the forest, allowing the trees and their roots to stay put and, with the use of clay tiles, rainwater is still able to seep into the earth around the house.

The extensive use of glass highlights the surrounding nature, whether viewed from inside (this page) or reflected in the mirrored facades (previous pages).

With its light material touches built around existing trees, the courtyard feels like a natural clearing in the woods. It separates the two blocks of the Mexican vacation retreat.

Well-being is architectural and spiritual in this spa structure that emerges organically from the heart of the Morelos forest.

179

PRIVATE SPA IN TEPOZTLÁN

At the Private Spa in Tepoztlán, architecture melts into the background, allowing nature to speak for itself. The house, designed for an avid athlete, is buried deep within a thickly forested valley in Morelos, Central Mexico. Viewed from above, only the edges of a rooftop garden pierce through the dense green; the circular forms of the garden's seating areas hint at something ancient that has emerged from the ground like the surrounding trees themselves.

The whole building follows this circular motif, its floor plan wrapping around a central void with sloped stone walls that suggest a tomb or temple, more than a space for exercise. The central void is lit from above by a round skylight piercing the heart of the wellness center. Whether rain or shine, the skylight allows the outside in. The building radiates outward from this central point with a series of rooms for activities and relaxation. These include a gym, massage room, lockers, showers and bathrooms, a sauna, and a frigidarium—a cold room with a small pool. A tunnel bisects the whole ensemble, dipping softly beneath ground level.

Climbing the sloped exterior walls, one reaches the 66-foot- (20-meter-) diameter "dish" of a roof that perches atop the building. The roof acts as a giant impluvium that captures rainwater that is then filtered down into underground cisterns. Yet it is also an additional space for relaxation. Complete with open fires and a hot tub, the roof is designed to continue the theme of wellness found inside, albeit with a direct connection to the surrounding tree canopies. With its generous planting, the roof terrace seems to extend into the forest without interruption.

The roof acts as a giant dish that captures rainwater to be filtered into underground cisterns while serving as an additional space for relaxation.

A tunnel bisects the whole spa ensemble, drawing visitors gently beneath ground level. The central void (left) is lit from above by a round skylight.

PRIVATE SPA IN TEPOZTLÁN

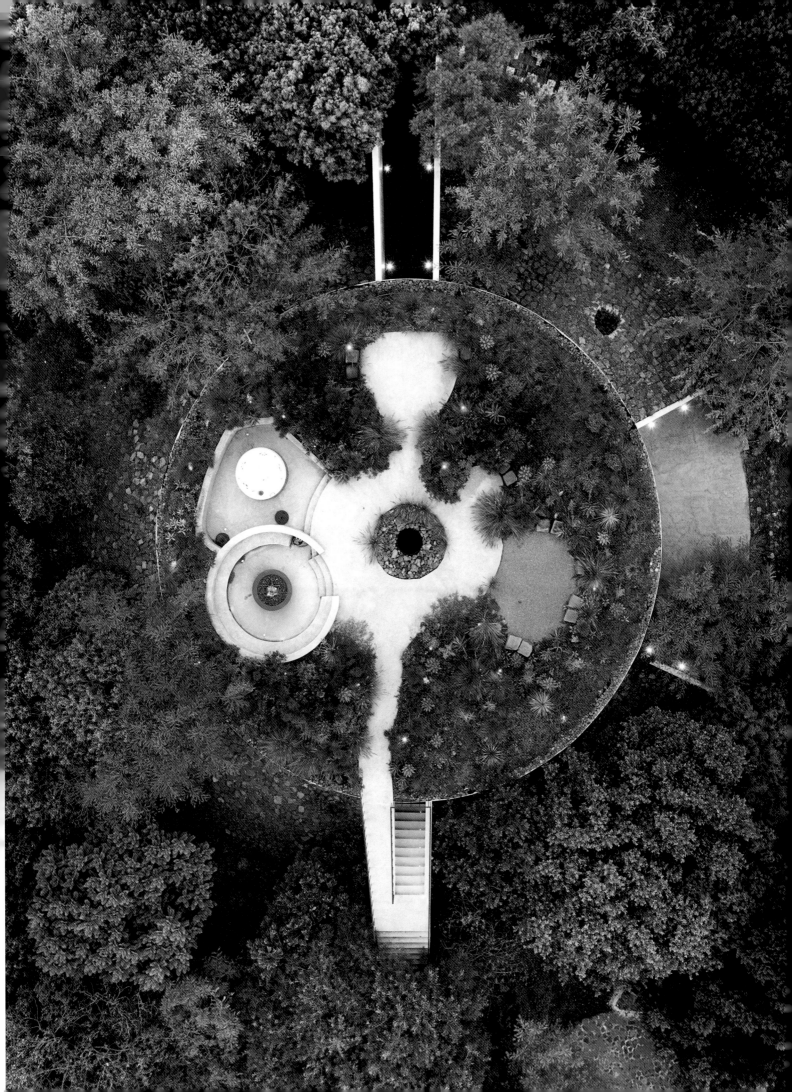

185 PRIVATE SPA IN TEPOZTLÁN

Combining stark
materiality and
a poetic approach
to domesticity, this
minimal haven in
Morelia is nestled into
the crest of a hill.

Sometimes a house need only be a ripple in the landscape. This unique property by HW Studio nudges its highest point above the natural contours of the central Mexican landscape like a grassy knoll. Viewed on approach, the turfed green roof of the house appears more like the forest floor than the apex of a concrete structure and reveals little of the quiet interior that it shelters.

The Hill in Front of the Glen was designed with a linear floor plan defined by two parallel exterior walls made of exposed concrete and floor-to-ceiling glass. The entrance to the house is accessed via an exterior open-air hallway that slices through the center of the structure with a paved slope just wide enough for one person. This choreographed entrance anticipates the house's monastic interior, a minimal haven of warm wooden floors, sleek polished concrete, and subtle steel profiles. The material palette echoes the surrounding forest: the aroma of the wooden floors blends with the trees; the steel will age like tree bark; and the concrete gives the house a monolithic atmosphere like a cave uncovered deep in the earth. This sensation is emphasized by the curve of the house's silhouette—a single archway creating one architectural swoop.

The arrangement of the rooms promotes varied experiences between interior seclusion and outward reflection: a bedroom's privacy is shielded by the undulating landscape, while common areas merge with the wooded scenery outside the floor-to-ceiling windows. The spaces are mostly interconnected without doorways, which reinforces the sense of the structure as one fluid experience, akin to the flow of nature. The house is a sanctuary for meditative seclusion and stillness amid the natural buzz of the forest and the rest of the world outside.

The monastic interior of the house is characterized by warm wooden floors and sleek polished concrete (above and right). The exterior open-air hallway slices through the center of the structure (opposite).

188

THE HILL IN FRONT OF THE GLEN

Natural and man-made worlds become inseparable at this solitary lakeside hideout, nestled deep within the Norwegian forest.

191

GJEMMESTED TELEMARK

When Gartnerfuglen Arkitekter says hideout, they mean it. Gjemmested Telemark is buried into a steep slope facing a small mountain lake in a secret location in southern Norway, and can only be accessed by boat in summer or on skis in winter when the lake is frozen. The hideout serves as a place to escape into nature—for fishing, lighting a fire, and disconnecting from technological distractions. It's a place designed for solitude, which disappears into its natural surroundings when it's not in use, even serving as a pitstop for thirsty birds on their way to the lake.

The hideout was constructed by carving rocks and scree out of the hillside and installing a timber skeleton clad with birch twigs. The twigs create a camouflaging effect while keeping an insulating layer of air beneath the snow. Entering through an "ear" of the hideout, visitors find an entrance room with a built-in desk: a place to work, think, and gaze at the surrounding nature. Heading further into the hideout, there is an open room with space for two people to lie down beneath a skylit tower, giving the space a chapel-like feel despite its tiny size. The textures of the natural exterior contrast with the clean white of the interior, heightening the properties of the Norwegian countryside outside and dramatizing the visual spectacle of the natural world.

Gjemmested Telemark features a timber skeleton clad with birch twigs. Visitors to the hideout enter through an "ear" (left) that leads to a small entrance room.

Local materials and
spectacular views
combine at these
rammed-earth villas
that float above the
Costa Rican jungle.

Like apparitions, the twin villas of Achioté float above the jungle at Bahía Ballena in southern Costa Rica. Designed by Czech architects Formafatal to be rented as vacation homes, the structures are defined by presence and absence—a combination of light material touches and extraordinary views across the bay toward the Pacific Ocean.

From the outside, visitors see rectilinear forms cast in natural creams, rusty reds, and earthy browns that make the villas seem at home among the verdant foliage. Exterior walls are either floor-to-ceiling windows, emphasizing the jungle and the sea beyond, or cast in rammed earth. The earth removed from the jungle floor for the foundations was repurposed to make the walls by pounding it into molds. This was the first use of rammed earth in Costa Rica, and the technique allowed the project to have a low environmental impact because no additional environmentally damaging materials were required to make the walls.

In addition to being structurally sound and aesthetically complementary, the thick walls help to cool the inside of the villas, which deliberately do not have air conditioners to reduce energy consumption. What's more, the villas collect rainwater for irrigation purposes and for use in the infinity pools that perch on the edge of the concrete floor plate. This connection to the surrounding environment is compounded by the seamless blurring of indoor and outdoor spaces. Floor-to-ceiling windows establish a never-ending visual connection to the jungle, while bedrooms are virtually terraces with beds (and obligatory mosquito nets). Together, the villas form an ensemble of contextually sensitive materiality and smart environmental design that are almost as impressive as the views out the windows.

The twin Achioté vacation homes appear to float above the jungle at Bahía Ballena in southern Costa Rica, overlooking the Pacific Ocean.

ACHIOTÉ

The thick walls (right) help keep the villa cool, eliminating the need for air-conditioning and reducing energy consumption. The bedrooms are virtually terraces with beds.

201

Moveable floor-to-ceiling windows in the villas' bedrooms create a constant visual connection with the surrounding jungle and the sea beyond.

With identical footprints, heights,
and raw materials, these jewel
boxes are naturally discrete yet
boldly transparent.

The Atherton Pavilions are the latest additions to a gradually expanding plot owned by a growing family in the San Francisco Bay Area. The two structures—one designed for use as an outdoor kitchen and dining space, the other as a meditation and workout room—are considered to be part of the landscape, which features a regionally characteristic blend of redwoods and other mature trees. The pavilions are therefore designed to be partially transparent and discrete, treading lightly and blending as seamlessly as possible with the natural surroundings.

Feldman Architecture achieved this blending effect through material choices for the pavilions, which include Alaskan Yellow Cedar slats on the facade and wooden trellis screens on either side of both structures. The screens create both a sense of privacy for the workout pavilion and a feeling of openness in the kitchen pavilion. The wooden features will show signs of weathering and aging as the pavilions go through seasons of use, becoming more integrated with the landscape as they do so.

Several landscaping elements unify the two pavilions, including a new water feature and decks. The kitchen pavilion acts as an extension of the pool and an outdoor lounge area. The outdoor kitchen includes a pizza oven, grill, and extensive storage. Both pavilions are slightly lifted above the landscape, giving the impression they are floating, further emphasizing the lightness of the architectural creations on the land below.

Through material choices, which include Alaskan Yellow Cedar slats on the facade, the pavilions are designed to blend as seamlessly as possible with their natural surroundings.

207

Several landscaping elements unify the two pavilions. One is a meditation and workout space (this page), and the other is an outdoor kitchen and dining area (opposite).

ATHERTON PAVILIONS

The Australian land-
scape rolls through
this Neo-Brutalist
bunker that blurs the
boundary between
inside and out.

For all its expressive and refined board-formed concrete set at rectilinear angles, Bunkeren is as much a project of sensitive landscaping as of Neo-Brutalist architecture. Located in a suburb of Newcastle in southwestern Australia, Bunkeren is a five-bedroom home and studio designed for a couple and their four young children. From outside, the dominant form of the building is the flat concrete roofs that form a cluster of platforms descending toward Dudley Beach. Beneath these roofs, a series of boxy volumes contain the living spaces of this dynamic home, with different units for main living spaces, children's bedrooms, study, kitchen, storage spaces, and more.

This sprawl of domestic containers mirrors one of the project's key ideas: the uninterrupted presence of the landscape's natural flow through the site. The house is integrated into the hillside to allow the coastal headland to dominate the experience of the site. Each room acts as its own ground floor, such that moving through the house one is never separated from the contours of the hillside. "I really like the idea of making the ground plane ambiguous, and so you're sort of half in the land and half on it," explains architect James Stockwell.

This sensation is emphasized with design elements that bring the landscape into the home in dramatic ways. The post-tensioned concrete structure allows for generous cantilevers that naturally blur the boundary between sheltered interior and open exterior. What's more, the exposed areas, including the flat roofs, flourish with endemic plants that bring bird and insect life and build pathways to the surrounding forest. This ecologically attentive approach extends to the building's environmental performance. The thermal mass of the concrete allows for passive cooling during the intense heat of summer, and the house runs on autonomous energy and water systems.

The five-bedroom home and studio is integrated into the Australian hillside, which makes itself known by erupting into the living spaces.

212

The thermal mass of concrete used at the Neo-Brutalist building allows for passive cooling during the intense heat of summer.

A stunning boutique hotel in southern
Mexico draws on diverse inspirations for
its geometric architectural acrobatics.

Nestled in the serene landscape of La Punta Zicatela in the state of Oaxaca in southern Mexico is Casa TO. With its prominent exposed concrete ziggurats, this boutique hotel was designed by Ludwig Godefroy to serve as a contemporary interpretation of an Oaxacan temple. As well as Mexican influences, it draws inspiration from other historical works of spectacular water-based architecture, such as the Basilica Cistern in Istanbul and the Hornsey Wood Reservoir in London. This inspiration is clearest with the extraordinary swimming pool, which runs through the center of a covered communal relaxation area, through circular concrete forms, and beneath the concrete bleachers that ascend from one side.

The hotel spans 6,500 square feet (600 square meters) and runs across nine suites, which are characterized by rigorous design, privacy, and sustainability, complete with natural finishes and handmade furniture. The hotel operates with environmental responsibility as a priority. It maintains a zero-plastic policy, treats wastewater for irrigation, and utilizes solar panels for energy. This commitment extends to Glou Glou, the hotel's restaurant, where a dialogue between original recipes and organic wines creates a sustainable culinary experience.

Spectacular concrete forms inspired by traditional Oaxacan architecture run throughout the boutique hotel in La Punta Zicatela.

An extraordinary swimming pool,
which draws inspiration from historical
cisterns (below), occupies the center
of a covered communal relaxation area.

This cave-like home is buried in the landscape, referencing ancient human dwellings alongside modern construction techniques.

The intention of Casa Orgánica was to create a space adapted to the innate environmental, psychological, and physical needs of a human. Its designer, Javier Senosiain, took inspiration from the origins of shelter, including the maternal cloister, animal dens, and early cave dwellings. Across these examples is a shared sense of welcoming curvaceous spaces similar to the cradle of a mother's embrace; cozy and integrated spaces that cater to the natural rhythms of human life.

The completed house is a family home that features spaces for cohabiting—a living room, dining room, and kitchen—and a sleeping area—with a dressing room and bathroom. The floor of the house is covered with a sand-colored carpet to bring the house aesthetically closer to the earth, and the tone is repeated across the walls and ceiling, creating a cave-like chromatic continuity. The rooms flow into each other with plasticity, facilitated by the use of ferro-cement—every inch is curved, giving the home a persistent sense of movement.

These interior spaces are, however, held within the cocoon of the landscape and barely visible from outside. The home seems folded inside the grassy hills of its site, accessed by following a spiral and tunnel that give the sensation of entering the earth to encounter the living, eating, and cooking spaces, followed eventually by the sleeping area.

The earthy tones, curvaceous structures, and built-in elements are a nod to ancient cave-like dwellings. The floor is covered with a sand-colored carpet.

With its large curved windows and skylights, the home remains surprisingly bright and connected to its landscape. The windows were oriented toward the best views.

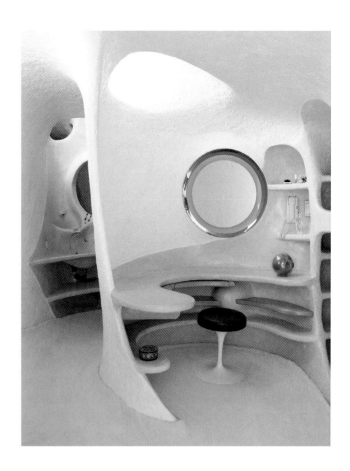

229

Casa Orgánica is folded inside the grassy hills of its Mexican site and can be accessed by following a tunnel inside.

CASA ORGÁNICA

Abstract, angular, and artistic, this quirky garden pavilion brings a flash of red to the Belgian countryside.

234

Refuge is a red concrete pavilion situated in the verdant garden of a family home in suburban Flanders. Both expressive in form and sensitive to its surroundings, the structure—which accompanies a main house—sits on a raised plinth that leaves the natural ground beneath it untouched by the swooping beams, calm pools, and open entrances of the pavilion. These doorways both frame the surrounding tall trees and shrubbery, and provide access to the studio and swimming pond held within. Those going for a dip will be surrounded by a fragmented *hortus conclusus* (enclosed garden), a semicircular beam, and half-finished walls that leave little separation between the unkempt landscape and the refined red finishes of Refuge. The circular form riffs on the idea of a clearing in a forest, again playing on the peculiar tension between presence and absence at the heart of this curious structure.

Despite its particular uses, Refuge was designed with repurposing in mind. The red concrete shell was completed with an interior finish that can be altered for future uses. The different building elements are not glued together, meaning they can be easily dismantled for a different construction, and the building fixtures were carefully selected from a demolished office site. Similarly, the structure is autonomous and off-grid. It receives power from solar panels in the main house and has its own heat pump as well as a self-contained sewage system.

Refuge, a red concrete garden pavilion in suburban Flanders, features a persistent and poetic interplay between absence and presence.

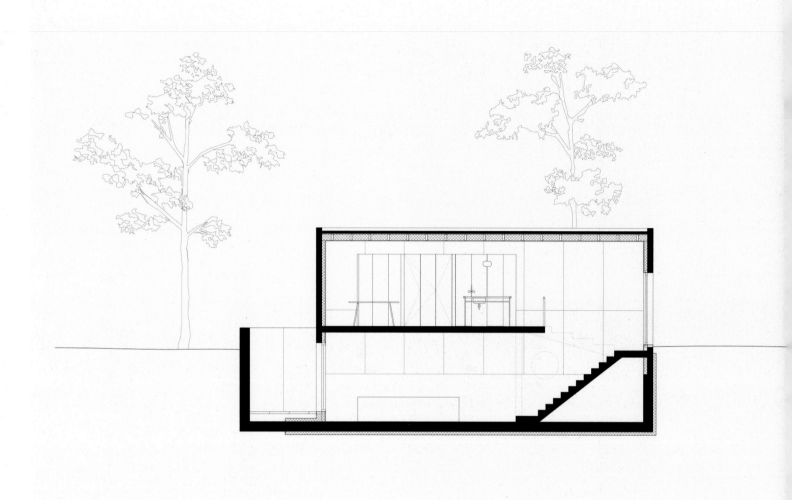

The concrete shell has minimal interior finishes, allowing for future, as yet unknown, uses. The different building elements can be easily dismantled for a different construction.

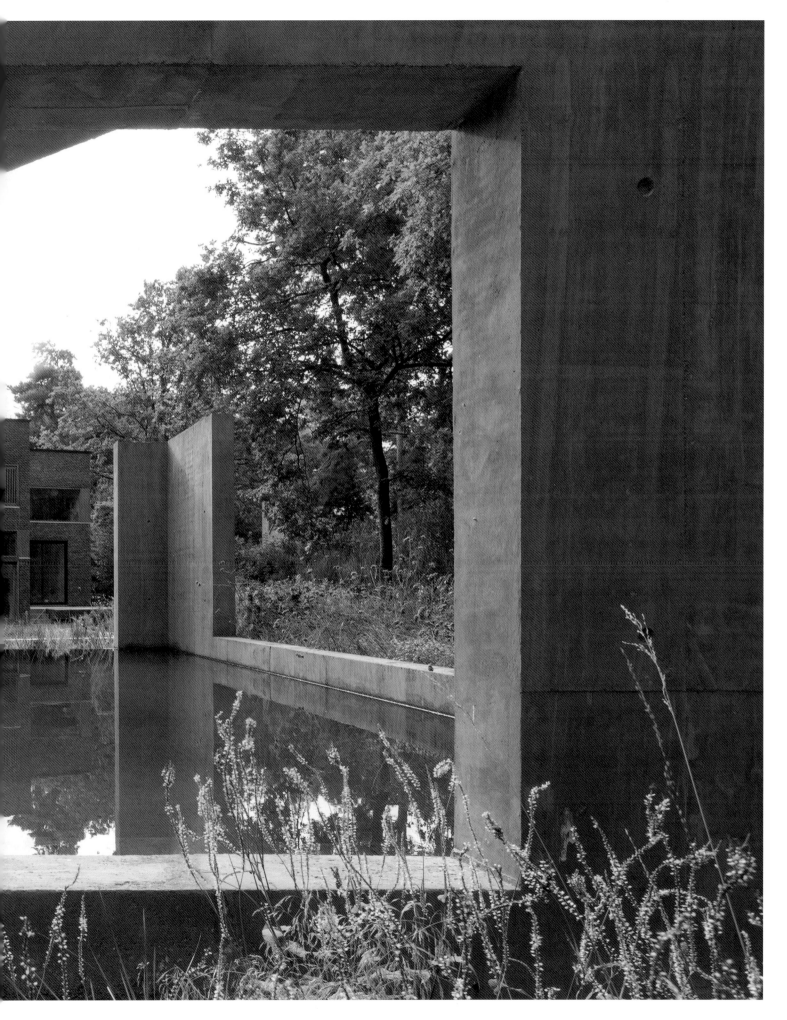

239 REFUGE

A modern farmhouse sits quietly on the coastal landscape, its disparate volumes held together by a cool central courtyard.

242

Abstracting the traditional forms of an Australian farmhouse, this house has an elegant confidence that allows it to sit comfortably among its coastal surroundings. With expansive outdoor areas and generous views toward the sea from the top of its hill, Merricks Farmhouse is architecturally subtle, designed like a lens to take in the surrounding landscape.

Capitalizing on the Australian climate, a courtyard acts as the house's center of gravity, tying together a cluster of otherwise disparate volumes contained beneath a low roof with deep eaves. For example, the front volume features all the main living spaces and functions as a simple one-bedroom pavilion. The courtyard features ponds and mature trees, as well as a communal table and stepping stones through the water—a striking blend of natural landscaping and domestic pleasures.

The house's interior is characterized by a feeling of shelter as well as frequent turns to the exterior. Large windows, skylights, and expansive doorways connect the house to its surroundings as if the landscape were unimpeded by the presence of the structure. This sensation is heightened by the environmentally light-touch operation of the home—domestic water is collected in a circular concrete tank rather than drawn from mains systems, and meter-thick walls help to keep the interior cool in the summer and warm in the winter. These walls also create a comfortable sense of enclosure and moments of intimacy amid the vastness of the 50-acre (20-hectare) property with its views over vineyards toward Phillip Island and Western Port Bay.

A verdant courtyard with ponds and mature trees is a central point of the Merricks Farmhouse, which features a large open-plan living room and six bedrooms.

A circular cement pool (below) mimics an agricultural water storage tank, a motif that is repeated in smaller court-yard pools. Large windows connect the house to its surroundings (opposite).

MERRICKS FARMHOUSE

MERRICKS FARMHOUSE

A smorgasbord of terraces is peppered
across the natural landscape of this home,
set amid the Santa Lucia mountainscape.

Arroyo Sequoia is a house that sits confidently amid the Santa Lucia mountains of Central California, its horizontal thrust contrasting with the upward reaches of its surrounding oak trees. The rest of the project is, however, highly sensitive to the surrounding topography and natural textures. The L-shaped plan allows it to settle naturally into the contours of the land. It is split between two structures, each completing one arm of the "L." This split separates the main living spaces from the bedrooms, while leaving an abundance of outdoor living space. Numerous large open terraces for outdoor gathering create clear vistas of the rolling hills surrounding the house. One terrace features an outdoor fireplace; another has an open fire pit.

The project's materiality is intentionally subdued, ensuring that the prominent focus remains on the natural beauty of the West Coast. The structure of the house features concrete, weathered steel, and cedar timber boarded walls and flooring, as well as floor-to-ceiling windows, allowing panoramic views of the hills, wildlife, and valley beyond.

A range of sustainability techniques were employed in the project. Stone for the terraces was sourced locally and the pollinators and other native plants of the site's meadows were restored as part of the landscape design processes. What's more, the garden was constructed to have minimal grading to avoid disturbing the preexisting site, allowing the oak woodland to be preserved and restored.

Arroyo Sequoia blends naturally into the contours of the land. Large open terraces surround a manicured inner courtyard with views of the surrounding hills.

250

The materiality of the project is deliberately restrained, allowing the oak woodland to take center stage.

The House of Green

Natural Homes and
Biophilic Architecture

This book was conceived, edited, and designed by gestalten.

Edited by Robert Klanten and Masha Erman

Editorial support by Effie Efthymiadi

Introduction by Carlo Ratti (pp. 8—11)
Features by Ashley D. Penn (pp. 82—87)
and Victoria Jackson & Rosa Isaacs (pp. 126—131)
Preface, project texts, and captions by George Kafka

Editorial Management: Arndt Jasper
Photo Editor: Zoe Paterniani

Design, layout, and cover by Stefan Morgner
Typeface: Fragment by Francesca Bolognini and Mat Desjardins

Cover image: Garden Tower House by Studio Bright
Photography: Rory Gardiner, rory-gardiner.com
Backcover image: Casa Orgánica by Javier Senosiain
Photography: Anna Dave, annadave.com

Printed by DZS Grafik d.o.o., Ljubljana, Slovenia
Made in Europe

Published by gestalten, Berlin 2024
ISBN 978-3-96704-140-8

For more information, and to order books, please visit www.gestalten.com

Bibliographic information published by the Deutsche Nationalbibliothek. The Deutsche Nationalbibliothek lists this publication in the Deutsche Nationalbibliografie; detailed bibliographic data is available online at www.dnb.de

None of the content in this book was published in exchange for payment by commercial parties or designers; the inclusion of all work is based solely on its artistic merit.

This book was printed on paper certified according to the standards of the FSC®.

ROSA ISAACS is a Design and Material Strategist from Aotearoa, now working in Brighton, U.K., at Oliver Heath Design, a world leader in biophilic design practices. With a particular interest in innovative biophilic and vernacular materials and design processes, she has consulted on a range of projects within the built environment from independent clothing brands to global hotel chains. She has also co-authored whitepapers in collaboration with Interface, Inc. and Schneider Electric.

VICTORIA JACKSON is Lead Researcher and Biophilic Design Strategist at Oliver Heath Design. With a particular focus on regenerative design, she consults on design projects, writes thought leadership papers, and creates courses to promote knowledge development within the built environment sector. In collaboration with Interface, Inc., she co-authored the *Creating Positive Spaces* design guides series for architects and designers. She also co-authored *Design a Healthy Home* and has had articles published by the *Journal of Biophilic Design* and Taylor and Francis's *Cities & Health* journal.

GEORGE KAFKA is a writer, editor, and curator based in London. He writes regularly on architecture, design, and ecology for publications including *The Architectural Review, e-flux,* and *Bauwelt.* He is currently the Future Observatory Curator at the Design Museum.

ASHLEY D. PENN was originally trained in horticulture before specializing in landscape architecture. He has worked in the architectural industry in the U.K. and Finland for many years and has written for online and print media on subjects including architecture, urban planning, landscape, and gardening.

CARLO RATTI, an architect and engineer by training, is Professor of the Practice of Urban Technologies at the Massachusetts Institute of Technology (MIT), where he directs the SENSEable City Lab and is a founding partner of the international design and innovation office Carlo Ratti Associati. A leading voice in the debate on the impact of new technologies on urban life and design, Carlo has co-authored over 500 publications, most recently the *Atlas of the Senseable City* (with Antoine Picon). His articles and interviews have appeared in international media such as the *New York Times,* the *Wall Street Journal,* the *Washington Post, Financial Times, Corriere della Sera, Il Sole 24 Ore,* and *Domus.* He also holds a Distinguished Professorship at Politecnico di Milano and is currently co-chairing the World Economic Forum's Global Future Council on Cities and Urbanization.